"Then they fasted that day, and put on sackcloth, and cast ashes upon their heads, and rent their clothes, and laid open the book of the law, wherein the heathen had sought to paint the likeness of their images." – 1 Maccabees 3:48

Undeniable
Full Color Evidence of Black Israelites In The Bible

Copyright © 2019 – Dante Fortson

Website: www.blackhistoryinthebible.com

ISBN: 9781692492786

First Edition.

Author: Dante Fortson

Dedication

This book is dedicated to every black person that has ever been told that there's no proof that Israel was black or that we're pushing a race based agenda based on misinterpreting scripture. The overwhelming evidence proves that not only are we 100% correct in our reading of scripture, but all over the world, non black people worshiped, and in some cases still worship a black Christ.

It is my sincere belief that by coupling physical evidence with scripture, that we will be able to wake up many of our brothers and sisters that are still lost in the lie of Eurocentric Christianity and the image of a European Jesus. While I personally do not teach race based salvation, the truth about who is who in scripture is important when it comes to interpretation of scripture. I pray that this book becomes a go-to resource in your fight for the truth.

"And ye shall know the truth, and the truth shall make you free." – John 8:32

Thank You

First I want to thank my parents, family, and close friends that have supported this journey from the very beginning. I want to give an extra special thanks to all of my Patrons for your continued support. Thank you to everyone that continues to read and support the BHITB website. Your sharing of studies, your questions, and your sharing of information is what made this book possible. Last and certainly not least, I want to thank TEOTW Ministries. We've been in this fight together for nearly a decade and it's been an honor debating, studying, and fellowshipping with you brothers over the truth of the word.

The Journey

When I started this journey in 2014, it was originally to discredit the belief that black people in America were the true Israelites of the Bible. At the time I was still caught up in the European deception that Israel was in the land, and many of the prophecies had been fulfilled. It was through researching the lineage of Ham that I came to believe that not only was Israel black, but that Israel had been intentionally targeted and brought to American during the Transatlantic Slave Trade.

There has never been any agenda for my ministry other than the truth, and I've been committed to sticking to the truth no matter how controversial it gets. I've never backed down from the truth because it was unpopular or in several cases cost me lots of regular readers. Minister Fortson.com was where this journey begin, but the Most High has shifted my ministry to reaching out to our people with the truth, and sharing that truth has led to BHITB becoming one of the largest sites in this field of research.

Understanding who we are as a people, why we were targeted for slavery, and why a loving God would allow this to happen to black people has all been made clear through understanding the scriptures as intended. I hope that the evidence presented in this book gives you the faith and boldness to speak up for the truth about scripture... and the truth is that the Most High chose us over every nation, chose our ancestors to write a message from HIM to us, and promises to return to save us from our current oppression again.

> "Behold, I will make them of the synagogue of Satan, which say they are Jews, and are not, but do lie; behold, I will make them to come and worship before thy feet, and to know that I have loved thee." - Revelation 3:9

UNDENIABLE

The claim that there is no evidence of a black Israel are always made by people that haven't bothered to look for any of the evidence. They will often repeat what they've been told to believe, but the truth is that there is lots of evidence both Biblically and historically that back up why many of us believe Israel was and still is black. The reason people are confused about the true Identity of Israel is because of the Renaissance Period, during which they painted and re-painted everyone white, while also hiding away or destroying other images of black apostles, prophets, and even Christ. The evidence presented in this book comes from real historical sources and can be verified by using Google, a map, and a Bible. All evidence appearing in this book is organized by date.

The Elamite Empire

One of the most interesting mysteries in the Bible surrounds the sons of Noah and the origin of each nation on the planet. According to most mainstream Christian researchers the sons of Noah divided into the nations as follows:

- Ham: Black Africans + Black Arabs
- Shem: "Olive" Hebrews + "Olive" Arabs
- Japheth: Europeans + Asians

However, discoveries of Biblical sites such as Shushan Palace in Susa are starting to paint an entirely different picture than the one presented to the general public by the church and media. According to the Bible, Elam was one of the sons of Shem:

The children of Shem; Elam, and Asshur, and Arphaxad, and Lud, and Aram." – Genesis 10:22

1549 - 1292 B.C. – 18th Egyptian Dynasty

One of the biggest false claims in our present time is that Egyptians were white, even though all evidence points to the contrary. We can see with our eyes that Egyptians were not Caucasian, did not paint themselves as Caucasian, nor were they ever described as anything other than black people.

- Caucasians did not come from the line of Ham.
- Caucasians would not paint themselves as black people.
- Caucasians would never name their country KMT (Kemet), which means "land of the blacks".

Even though there is zero evidence to support the claim of a white Egypt, people still believe it. Thankfully, there is tons of evidence available to support the fact the Egyptians were black. One of the biggest treasure troves of proof comes from the 18th Dynasty of Egypt. The tomb of Rekhmara is filled with paintings of black Egyptians and black Hebrews on the wall. Europeans have known about these images for centuries, but that hasn't stop them from misrepresenting the truth.

Tomb of Rekhmire – 18th Dynasty

A very common claim among non believers is that there is no evidence of Israel ever having been in Africa, and certainly not in Egypt as slaves.

The previous picture represents Israelites making bricks while Egyptian overseers make sure they get their work done. Perhaps the most interesting confirmation that the above picture represents Israelite slaves, is a modern fake created by Europeans that had knowledge of the original.

There are quite a few similarities in the pictures that let us know that the recreation is an intentional deception that was commissioned and then placed in some Bibles to deceive believers. The following similarities appear in both the original and the European remake.

- The way the bricks are laid out on the ground.
- The man digging into the ground with his "A" shaped tool.
- The man carrying a single large rock or stone on his shoulder.
- The man pouring water out of the pot.
- The device used to carry multiple cut blocks of stone.

All of this evidence adds up to an intentionally deceptive picture that was commissioned to perpetuate a false idea of what Israelites looked like. Even more sinister is the fact that Bibles are usually assembled by organizations or groups of people, which means that an entire group of people conspired to insert this fake picture into the backs of Bibles instead of just using the original.

Pharaoh Akhenaten – King Tut's Father

Dura-Europos synagogue painting: Moses and the Hebrews crossing the Red Sea, pursued by Pharoah: 303 B.C. - 256 A.D.

In the image above, we see Moses and the drowning of the Egyptians. They are all depicted as black people, which also confirms the scripture in which Moses was mistaken for an Egyptian.

"Now the priest of Midian had seven daughters: and they came and drew *water*, and filled the troughs to water their father's flock. And the shepherds came and drove them away: but Moses stood up and helped them, and watered their flock. And when they came to Reuel their father, he said, How *is it that* ye are come so soon to day? And they said, An Egyptian delivered us out of the hand of the shepherds, and also drew *water* enough for us, and watered the flock." – Exodus 2:16-19

In addition to confirming Moses' dark appearance, the painting also confirms the early belief that God is black. We see his arms coming down from the sky just over Moses. The description is also reflected in the Bible in the book of Revelation:

"And he that sat was to look upon like a jasper and a sardine stone: and *there was* a rainbow round about the throne, in sight like unto an emerald." – Revelation 4:3

Jasper Stones

Rainbow Jasper Stones

Sardis / Sardine Stone

By looking at the color of the stones, we know that both John and the painter were intentionally describing a brown skinned Creator.

From the Bristol Psalter, believed to be a Byzantine Psalter written in the 11th century in ancient Greek. The Psalter has 14 odes and the apocryphal Psalm 151. The exact provenance is unknown. Described as an Unnoticed Byzantine Psalter in a 1921 magazine article.
Image f. 7v: King David with his musicians.

"And he sent, and brought him in. **Now he *was* ruddy, *and* withal of a beautiful countenance**, and goodly to look to. And the LORD said, Arise, anoint him: for this *is* he." — 1 Samuel 16:12

Raw Unpolished Rubies

Red / Ruddy Heifer

Red / Ruddy People

The Oldest Known Depiction of Christ
Coptic Museum – Cairo, Egypt

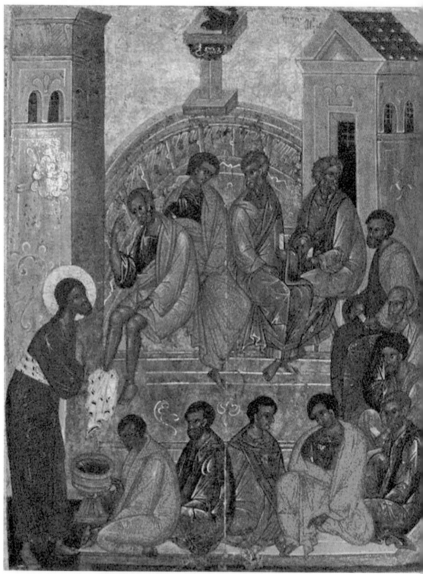

Christ washing the feet of the Disciples.
Icon of Pskov School. 16th century.

The Crowning of The King of Judah

Ethiopian Icons of Black Israelites

55 A.D. – 117 A.D. - Tacitus

Tacitus was a Roman historian that lived during the lifetime of the apostle Paul. While he did not create any images of Israelites, his testimony that Israelites looked like Egyptians and Ethiopians, serves to confirm why Paul was mistaken for an Egyptian in Acts 21:38. It also adds clarity to The Most High comparing Israelites to Ethiopians in Amos 9:7.

"A few authorities hold that in the reign of Isis the surplus population of Egypt was evacuated to neighboring lands under the leadership of Hierosolymus and Judas. Many assure us that the Jews are descended from those Ethiopians who were driven by fear and hatred to emigrate from their home country when Cepheus was king. There are some who say that a motley collection of landless Assyrians occupied a part of Egypt, and then built cities of their own, inhabiting the lands of the Hebrews and the nearer parts of Syria..." – Tacitus, Histories 5.2-5

Because Tacitus is cited as a credible European source, his words are important in understanding that belief in black Israelites is not new, nor is it exclusively associated with Black Hebrew Israelite camps.

70 A.D. – Israelites Flee Into Africa

"The black Jews who migrated to the Sudan from the North converged with the Jews migrating from the eastern Sudan to the countries of the Niger River...There is much proof, and still much more to be revealed by scholars, that there existed prior to the slave trade and subsequent to it many tribes, colonies, and kingdoms in West Africa." – Rudolf R. Windsor, Babylon To Timbuktu (pg. 120)

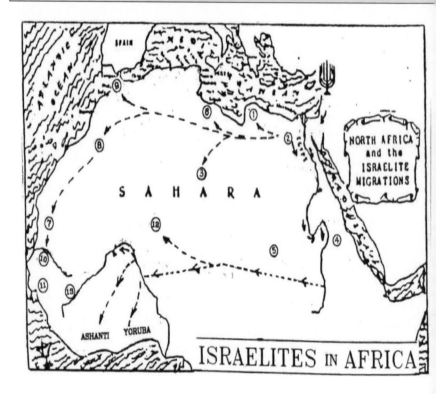

The true Israelites were scattered in all directions. The slaves that were brought to America are descendants of those Israelites that were disbursed into Africa, many, many years ago (about 2,500 years ago).

1. CYRENE – 125 c.e.; Israelites attempt to establish a Hebrew African Empire. Roman suppression forces further Israelite migrations into Africa.

2. ELEPHANTINE – 600 b.c.e.; Israelites establish a garrison. 70 c.e., Romans conquer and enslave over 100,000 Israelites.

3. TAMENTIT – 1492 c.e.; Ottoman Moslems destroy a 1,000 year old Hebrew settlement.

4. ETHIOPIA – 955 b.c.e.; Menelik, son of Solomon and the queen of Sheba, establishes an Israelite dynasty that lasted almost 3,000 years.

5. UGANDA – Line of 33 kings tracing their lineage to King David (Uganda tradition).

6. LIBYA – 640 c.e.; Israelite queen Diah Cahena organizes an army to defend against Roman and Arab incursions into North Africa.

7. KAZEMBE – 1831 c.e.; Shemitic Africans who's king wears the Mitre Headwrap resembling that of the Israelite High Priest.

8. MARRAKESH – 1000 c.e. to 1500 c.e.; Hebrews allowed to practice the Torah (Islamic period).

9. TANGIER – 1150 c.e.; Israelite sanctuary established by Beni-Moussa (sons of Moses).

10. KAMNURIA – Medieval Hebrew State north of the Senegal River.

11. GHANA – 300 c.e.; Hebrew dynasty established by Za El Yemeni lasts about 1,000 years: finally known as the Songhay Empire.

12. LAMLAM – 12th century Hebrew kingdom, "200 miles east of Timbuktu" (Al Edrisi).

13. NIGER RIVER – circa 1850 c.e.; "seven Princes descending from the kings of the ancient Israelites" (Fettasi tradition).

800 A.D. – The Tribe of Dan In Africa

"While it was regarded as merely a myth for many years – appearing in several written and oral versions – something striking occurred in the year 880 C.E. that left an imprint on Jewish consciousness for centuries to come. One day, a small, very dark-skinned Jew named Eldad showed up in the Jewish community of Kairouan, in modern-day Tunisia, claiming to be descended from the Tribe of Dan. He related fascinating accounts of the life and customs of this majority of the Jewish people that had disappeared. Of particular interest was the knowledge he claimed to have of early religious law and the archaic Hebrew that he spoke. From this point onward, the existence of the 10 Lost Tribes was regarded as a fact, as something whose validity could be tested in reality.

Where do the lost tribes reside? Perhaps in Central Asia or equatorial Africa?" – Haaretz, September 4, 2013

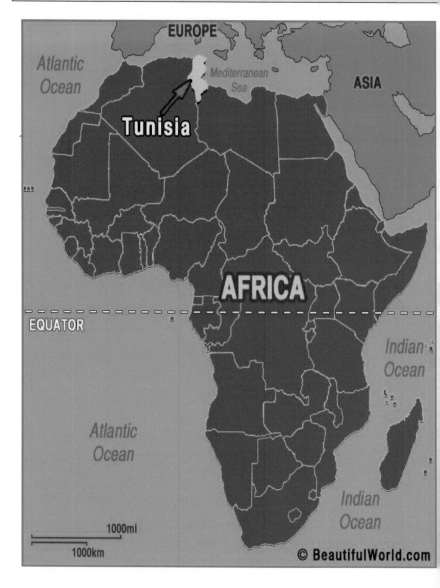

1300s A.D. – Daniel The Prophet

Daniel the Prophet - 14th Century, (Byzantine Museum, Athens)

1400s A.D. – Black Jews Deported

Barbot states, that in the reign of Don John II., and about the close of the fifteenth century, large numbers of Jews were expelled from Portugal and taken to the coast of Southern Guinea, that the island of St. Thomas, which is not more than one hundred miles from the mainland, was populated by mulattoes descended from the Jewish exiles and Anglo women. It is possible that the Jewish type of character noticed at the Gabun and Loango may have originated from this source; but if so it is unknown to the present inhabitants of the country, and it would have been somewhat singular if the Roman Catholic missionaries at Loango had not detected this circumstance instead of regarding them as a pure African family of Jews.

Kongo and Angola or Dongo people.—There have been so many of the Kongos and Angolos brought to this country in former years, while still greater numbers have been imported into Brazil of late, that it scarcely seems necessary to give a very minute account of them in this place. It is important to remark, however, that these families in Africa cannot be fairly estimated by such specimens of the nation as have been brought to America; for the subjects of the slave trade have almost invariably been gathered either from certain degraded clans that are interspersed among the more powerful tribes, or from

According to the text, the Jews were expelled from Portugal and taken to the coast of Southern Guinea, which is located in West Africa. St. Thomas is located just off the coast of Africa, and currently has the name São Tomé and Príncipe. The descendants of the Jews living in São Tomé and Príncipe are described as "Mulatto". If you're not familiar with the term, it is a term used to describe a person mixed with black and white. Many people find the term to be offensive. However, it is a major piece of evidence because the writer points out that the women were Anglo (white). By process of elimination it means that the Jewish men spoken of in the text were black. The writer confirms that people in Gabon were most likely descended from black Hebrews. Gabon is located on the West Coast of Africa just like Guinea and it was the missionaries that first noticed that the people in Gabon and Loango were not just African Jews, but were different. Here are the related maps.

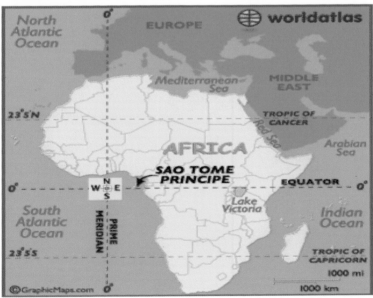

Following map shows where captured Israelites were taken from during the Transatlantic Slave Trade, which started in 1619.

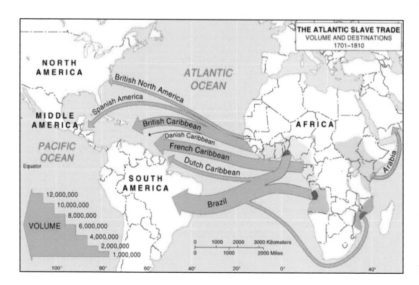

1510 – More Black Than Any Other Color

22   THE TRAVELS OF

THE CHAPTER CONCERNING A MOUNTAIN INHABITED BY JEWS.[1]

At the end of eight days we found a mountain which appeared to be ten or twelve miles in circumference, in which mountain there dwell four or five thousand Jews, who go naked, and are in height five or six spans, and have a feminine voice, <u>and are more black than any other colour.</u> They live entirely upon the flesh of sheep, and eat nothing else. They are circumcised, and confess that they are Jews; and if they can get a Moor into their hands, they skin him alive. At the foot of the said mountain we found a tank of water, which is water that falls in the rainy season. We loaded with the said water 16,000 camels, whereat the Jews were ill-pleased; and they went about that mountain like wild goats, and on no account would they descend into the plain, because they are mortal enemies of the Moors.

vol. ii. p. 118, *note.* See also Caussin de Perceval, *Histoire des Arabes avant l'Islamisme, etc.,* vols. ii. 641-644; iii. 193-201, 444. Niebuhr, *Déscription de l'Arabie,* pp. 326, 327.

Varthema evidently miscalculated the effects of distance in diminishing objects; hence, I presume, his fabulous measurement of the Jews at five or six spans in height, and his failing to see the scanty cloth round their loins, which still constitutes the only garment of the common Bedawin of the Hijàz. As to complexion, if those seen by our traveller were like the generality of the Jews in Yemen, he aptly describes it as " more black than any other colour." In that respect they are not to be distinguished from the Arab Bedawin.

Note: Ludovico uses the word Moor in place of Arab.

Ludovico di Varthema (c. 1470 – 1517), Itinerario de Ludouico de Varthema Bolognese, published in Rome in 1510.

1710 – 1766 A.D. - Judah In Africa

In the early to mid 1700s A.D., European cartographers (map makers) began noting that the Kingdom of Judah was located on the western coast of Africa, which is where the main focus of the Transatlantic Slave Trade was. The following maps show that Judah was located on the west coast of Africa, marked as "the slave coast" on many European maps. For full maps, please visit Black History In The Bible.com and click on the "Maps" tab. Judah, Iuda, Wida, Whiddah, and other variations of the name Judah appear on maps based upon which language the map is written in.

Composite Atlas. Amsterdam, Covens & Mortier, c. 1720

1737 Map of Judah On The West Coast of Africa

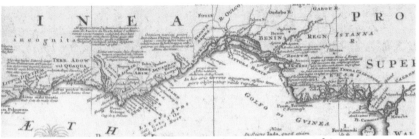

1743 Homann Heirs Map of Judah In West Africa

1766 Gift To The Duke of Orleans

Just above the west coast of Africa, and just below Nigritia (Negroland) on the map above, there is a note written which reads, "According to Edrifsithe the land hereabout was populated by Jews."

1969 – Memorandum To The President

In 1969 Henry Kissenger sent a memorandum to the president, in which he refers to the Igbo as "the wandering Jews of West Africa." Historically, we know that many of the people taken in the Transatlantic Slave Trade were of Igbo descent.

"Biafra (3, 000 sq. miles, 4-6 million). Colonel Ojukwu — 35, British-trained, erstwhile playboy — presides over the popular support and military morale of a people convinced that defeat means extinction. **The Ibos are the wandering Jews of West Africa** — gifted, aggressive, Westernized; at best envied and resented, but mostly despised by the mass of their neighbors in the Federation. They have fought well (by African standards) against heavy odds; their cynical public relations use of the starvation has been brilliant." – Henry Kissenger, (Tuesday, January 28, 1969 Memorandum for the president)

The full text of the memorandum can be found at The U.S. State Department website (online archive).

Zondervan: Negroes Aren't From Ham

Ham (hăm, perhaps **hot**). 1. The youngest son of Noah, born probably about 96 years before the Flood; and one of eight persons to live through the Flood. He became the progenitor of the dark races; not the Negroes, but the Egyptians, Ethiopians, Libyans and Canaanites (Gen. 10:6-20). His indecency, when his father lay drunken, brought a curse upon Canaan (Gen.

1985 - Cambridge University Press

Blacks and Jews: the same claim (The premisses of the movements)

In the first months of 1879 there was a massive migration of some 5000 Blacks to the Northern territories of the United States, mainly Kansas and Oklahoma. This exodus was of despairing Blacks seeking a refuge, a place where their political rights would mean something, where they would be free from economic exploitation and above all from the dangerous activities of the Klu Klux Klan. One of the members of this exodus was Benjamin Pap Singleton, an elderly and colourful man who lead a group of 300 Blacks to Cherokee county in Kansas. There they founded a colony, 'Singleton's colony', Singleton calling himself 'the Moses of the Exodus of coloured people'.

From 1900 onwards North and South Carolina were overrun by black preachers who were propagating a doctrine according to which the lost tribe of the House of Israel was none other than the Negroes. Although this might at first sight seem an odd claim it can be seen as reflecting the beliefs that some black slaves had held during their captivity when they were interrogated on their origins, their destiny. A historical example supports this hypothesis. A slave uprising took place in Richmond, Virginia, at the beginning of the nineteenth century which was led by a slave called Gabriel Prosser, an outstanding personality who had acquired some knowledge of the Bible. He frequently referred to it in order to convince his brothers that they were the descendants of the Israelites and that God would free them from slavery as he had their ancestors. He identified himself with Samson, his favorite Biblical character. Like Samson he wore his hair long, as a sign given by God of the Alliance made with his

220

The hypothesis of the existence of African Jewish communities

We know that the Jewish religion is one which is passed from parents to children and that it is the fundamental ingredient in the cohesion of the group. When one studies the Jewish religion it is clear how much it serves as the armature, the context for society. In the case of Black Judaism, the study of the significance of religious life in social life can help to rediscover traces of a more ancient Judaism that some African groups could have adopted and that could have been conserved by their slave descendants on American soil.

Were there black slaves who were Jewish through religion who maintained the faith of their ancestors after they had been forcibly transported to America? Only through an analysis of the mythology of the Jewish African origins of the Black Hebrews will this become clear. The following are the major sources that need to be considered in such an analysis: (a) witnesses, tales of the explorers who mention the existence of communities of Black Jews on the African continent and particularly in the areas where the slave ships picked up the black slaves; (b) rites and customs, which have more or less explicit analogies with those of Judaism; (c) the semantics and the dialectology of some African societies reveal some features comparable with those of Judaism; (d) the deductions and conclusions of anthropological and sociological work done in Africa.

It is well known that 1500 years before Islam, Judaism was present in Africa. Travellers' tales and the stories of journeys across North Africa, the Sahara and the Sudan provide considerable evidence of the existence of Jewish communities on the African continent. We know that from the time of saint Jerome (340-420) a chain of Jewish commercial towns stretched almost uninterrupted from Mauritania to India. St. Augustin learnt Hebrew in Tazem where there was

It is well known that 1500 years before Islam, Judaism was present in Africa. Travellers' tales and the stories of journeys across North Africa, the Sahara and the Sudan provide considerable evidence of the existence of Jewish communities on the African continent. We know that from the time of saint Jerome (340-420) a chain of Jewish commercial towns stretched almost uninterrupted from Mauritania to India. St. Augustin learnt Hebrew in Tazem where there was a Judaeo-Syrian colony which came from Cyrenicia. These groups went as far as Aoukar in the southern Sahara and, according to the chronicles of the Sudan, the dynasty of the kings of Ghana originated in this group. Jewish contacts and influences with Black Africa were also noted by the Arab geographers Ibn Khordadeb and El Bekri who stated that the routes of the trans-saharan trade, in which Jewish caravans and interpreters were involved, culminated in Ghana and

231

Page 231

In Southern Nigeria the natives call Black Jews the strange people on the Emo Yo Quaim. They are called the B'nai Ephraim the sons of Ephraim. They claim that their ancestors came from Morocco and this is supported by Godbey who noted that their language is a mixture of Maghrebian Arab, ancient Hebrew and local patois: for example *abu* meaning father became *yaba*, *umm* for mother is close to the Hebrew word. These Emo Yo Quaim Jews live in the ondo district and have a copy of the *Torah*.

The study of customs and rites and the analysis of the semantics of these African tribes have led many of their observers to propose some hypotheses and even to draw some conclusions. Doctor Allen H. Godbey reached the following conclusion: "These factors have a very specific significance if we consider the presence of Judaism among the American Negroes. Hundreds of thousands of slaves were transported to America from West Africa during the trade wich started some 400 years ago. What traces of Judaism still remained among the Negroes of West Africa at that period? To the extent that they were persecuted they were more likely than other Negroes to be seized during wars and sold as slaves. It is virtually certain that many part Jewish Negroes were among those sent as slaves to

235

Page 235

ULYSSES SANTAMARIA

America. How many of them would have been able to conserve some Jewish customs is another question. This conclusion put forward by Godbey, which argues for the existence of a more or less recurrent Judaism in West Africa in the same places as those from which the Negroes were taken, is shared by others, such as Maurice Delafosse. But most significantly it has been adopted by a class of educated Black Americans as a key argument to demonstrate that the Jewish religion is the traditional religion of Africans brought in slavery to the American continent.

Page 236

Unexplainable

When we lay out the historical evidence, it is undeniable that there has been a massive cover up of history. One of the most impressive facts about this journey is that the powers that be have been able to hide much of it without hiding it at all. It's written down in the Bible, sung in songs, and even referenced continuously without many of us even realizing it.

Skin Color In The Bible

The most obvious and often overlooked straightforward references to skin color are present in scripture. Too often, when asked about these occurrences, pastors will often respond as follows:

- It's not about race / skin color.
- The Bible doesn't mention skin color.
- They will try to find a way to explain away references to black skin as "ash poured on their skin during mourning or repentance. They may also claim that these were people with dark tans.

The following Bible verses contain direct references to Israel's skin color, some containing direct comparisons to other black objects to make the intent clear.

"**My skin is black upon me**, and my bones are burned with heat." – Job 30:30

"**I** *am* **black, but comely**, O ye daughters of Jerusalem, as the tents of Kedar, as the curtains of Solomon." – Song of Solomon 1:5

39

"Look not upon me, **because I *am* black**, because the sun hath looked upon me: my mother's children were angry with me; they made me the keeper of the vineyards; *but* mine own vineyard have I not kept." – Song of Solomon 1:6

"Judah mourneth, and the gates thereof languish; **they are black unto the ground**; and the cry of Jerusalem is gone up." – Jeremiah 14:2

"**Our skin was black like an oven** because of the terrible famine." – Lamentations 5:10

Mistaken For Hamites In The Bible

In Eurocentric Christian teaching, Ham is the father of the entire black race, but there is a major inconsistency when it comes to Egypt. Even though the Bible says Mizraim (Egypt) is the son of Ham, Eurocentric Christianity pivots on their position. They claim that Egyptians weren't black, even though their father was the father of all black people. The reason for that is because Israelites are both compared to and mistaken for Hamites throughout the entirety of scripture.

"**And all the house of Joseph, and his brethren, and his father's house: only their little ones, and their flocks, and their herds, they left in the land of Goshen.** And there went up with him both chariots and horsemen: and it was a very great company. And they came to the threshingfloor of Atad, which *is* beyond Jordan, and there they mourned with a great and very sore lamentation: and he made a mourning for his father seven days. **And when the inhabitants of the land, the Canaanites, saw the mourning in the floor of Atad, they said, This *is* a grievous mourning to the Egyptians:** wherefore the name of it was called Abelmizraim, which *is* beyond Jordan." – Genesis 50:8-11

"Now the priest of Midian had seven daughters: and they came and drew *water*, and filled the troughs to water their father's flock. And the shepherds came and drove them away: **but Moses stood up and helped them**, and watered their flock. And when they came to Reuel their father, he said, How *is it that* ye are come so soon to day? **And they said, An Egyptian delivered us out of the hand of the shepherds**, and also drew *water* enough for us, and watered the flock." – Exodus 2:16-19

"*Are* **ye not as children of the Ethiopians unto me**, O children of Israel? saith the LORD. Have not I brought up Israel out of the land of Egypt? and the Philistines from Caphtor, and the Syrians from Kir?" – Amos 9:7

"And **as Paul was to be led into the castle**, he said unto the chief captain, May I speak unto thee? Who said, Canst thou speak Greek? **Art not thou that Egyptian**, which before these days madest an uproar, and leddest out into the wilderness four thousand men that were murderers?" – Acts 21:37-38

Tomb of Nakht and his wife Tawy TT 52 Abd el-Qurna

Israelites Mixing With Hamites

According to Eurocentric Christianity and some Hebrew Israelite camps, Israel wasn't allowed to mix with anyone except for other Israelites. However, both are absolutely wrong. The Bible is clear that they did indeed mix with Hamites on a regular basis. The following chart shows all of the marriages between Hebrews and Hamites, and the children that resulted from the union.

- M = Married
- U = Unmarried

STATUS	MEN (Shemite)	WOMEN (Hamite)	CHILDREN (Mixed)	BIBLE Verses
M	Abraham	Hagar (Egyptian)	Ishmael	Genesis 16:15
M	David	Abigail (Carmelitess)	Daniel	1 Chronicles 3:1
M	David	Ahinoam (Jezreelitess)	Amnon	1 Chronicles 3:1
M	David	Bathsheba (Gilonite / Canaanite)	Solomon	2 Samuel 12:24
M	Esau	Adah (Hittite)	Eliphaz	Genesis 36:4
M	Esau	Bashemath (Hittite)	Reuel	Genesis 36:4
M	Esau	Judith (Hittite)	N/A	Genesis 26:34
M	Joseph	Asenath (Egyptian)	Ephraim Manasseh	Genesis 46:20
M	Judah	Daughter of Shuah	Er Onan	Genesis 38:2

		(Canaanite)	Shelah	
U	Judah	Tamar (Canaanite)	Pharez Zarah	Ruth 4:12
M	Moses	Ethiopian Woman (Ethiopian)	N/A	Numbers 12:1
U	Samson	Delilah (Philistine)	N/A	Judges 16:4
U	Samson	Prostitute (Philistine)	N/A	Judges 16:1
M	Simeon	Unnamed (Canaanite)	Shaul	Exodus 6:15
M	Solomon	Pharaoh's Daughter (Egyptian)	N/A	1 Kings 7:8
U	Solomon	Queen of Sheba (Ethiopian)	Menelik I	Ethiopian History

In addition to the above marriages where individuals are named, there are also other marriages mentioned between Israelites and Hamites, where no names are given.

'And **the son of an Israelitish woman, whose father *was* an Egyptian,** went out among the children of Israel: and this son of the Israelitish *woman* and a man of Israel strove together in the camp..." – Leviticus 24:10

'And **the children of Israel dwelt among the Canaanites,** Hittites, and Amorites, and Perizzites, and Hivites, and Jebusites: **And they took their daughters to be their wives, and gave their daughters to their sons,** and served their gods. And the children of Israel did evil in the sight of the LORD, and forgat the LORD their God, and served Baalim and the groves." – Judges 3:5-6

In every circumstance where God is angered about a marriage, it is not based on skin color, but by Israel adopting idolatry and worshiping other gods. There is nothing in the Bible that bases marriage on skin color. It is about idolatry, which is why there are Mosaic laws for non Israelites to convert to Judaism (religion / lifestyle). There is nothing in scripture that calls marriage between Hamites and Israelites a sin, but what is absent from the Bible are any accounts of Israelites marrying anyone from the line of Japheth.

Black Slaves Knew Hebrew

Many of us have heard and even sang *Kumbaya* at some point in our lives, but most people aren't aware of the origin of the song or the meaning of the words. When I was in elementary school, we were told that it meant "come by here", and that's what I and many others have believed for a long time.

- Did you know that that *Kumbaya* (*Kum-ba-yah*) is a Hebrew sentence?
- Did you know that it was sang in Gullah, which is a Hebrew word?

The History of Kumbaya (Kum-Ba-Yah)

According to history, the song was first recorded in the early 1920s. However, it is believed to have originated with Southern Slaves in the Gullah language. Gullah is a language that was spoken by slaves that inhabited North Carolina, South Carolina, Georgia, and Florida.

- Kumbaya Lyrics
- Kumbaya my Lord, kumbaya
- Kumbaya my Lord, kumbaya

- Kumbaya my Lord, kumbaya
- Oh Lord, kumbaya
- Someone's singing Lord, kumbaya
- Someone's singing Lord, kumbaya
- Someone's singing Lord, kumbaya
- Oh Lord, kumbaya
- Someone's laughing, Lord, kumbaya
- Someone's laughing, Lord, kumbaya
- Someone's laughing, Lord, kumbaya
- Oh Lord, kumbaya
- Someone's crying, Lord, kumbaya
- Someone's crying, Lord, kumbaya
- Someone's crying, Lord, kumbaya
- Oh Lord, kumbaya
- Someone's praying, Lord, kumbaya
- Someone's praying, Lord, kumbaya
- Someone's praying, Lord, kumbaya
- Oh Lord, kumbaya
- Someone's sleeping, Lord, kumbaya
- Someone's sleeping, Lord, kumbaya
- Someone's sleeping, Lord, kumbaya
- Oh Lord, kumbaya
- Oh Lord, kumbaya

Here is a breakdown of what the phrase *Kum-ba-yah* means in Hebrew.

The Meaning of Kumbaya

- **Kum (Qum):** Strong's #6965 - Stand up, arise
- **Ba:** Doesn't have any meaning alone in Hebrew, but may be an abbreviation for Abba, which means "father" (unconfirmed).
- **Yah:** Strong's #3050 - This word is translated as LORD in scripture when referring to the God of Israel.

Loosely translated, the lyrics seem to mean "arise father God" or "stand up father God" and NOT "come by here" as we've been fooled into believing. This was a cry for help from our ancestors to Yah to free them from slavery. Wikipedia does confirm this as well, although they do downplay the importance and connection to slavery:

> "The song was originally a simple appeal to God to come and help those in need." – Wikipedia

As with everything else we create, it was quickly appropriated into European culture. Europeans have an obsession with appropriating Hebrew culture. Part of the reason for concluding that the words are Hebrew in origin is due to the fact that it was sung in Gullah, which is also a Hebrew word.

Kumbaya Research From The Library of Congress

- https://www.loc.gov/folklife/news/pdf/FCNews32_3-4_opt.pdf
- https://blogs.loc.gov/folklife/2018/02/kumbaya-history-of-an-old-song/

Those links are a direct link to the Library of Congress website (loc.gov). Right there on the cover is a Hebrew newspaper with Hebrew writing on it. While they push fake European Jews throughout the "research", it does further confirm that we are indeed on the right track. Our people are Hebrews. What they don't explain is why black people taken from Africa and enslaved in America were crying out to the Hebrew God Yah to rescue them from slavery.

A Brief History of Gullah

Like many people my age or very close to it, I first became aware of Gullah through the TV series Gullah Gullah Island, which was one of the few shows on Nickelodeon that featured a majority black cast.

Every week they'd teach about Gullah culture and more. The United States government officially recognizes Gullah as a language consisting of Creole (French + English) and West African. It's the last part that that leads us back to the English slave trade map that shows The Kingdom of Judah located in West Africa.

The Meaning of Gullah

- **Gullah:** Strong's #1543 - basin, bowl, spring

The Gullah language is a mixture of languages, so the Hebrew word for bowl or basin is fitting, since those are typically used for mixing things together. All evidence points to *Kumbaya* being a Hebrew song created by descendants of Judah. There isn't any other explanation as to why black slaves would have so many connections to the language. It also serves as circumstantial evidence that slaves most likely spoke Hebrew when they arrived in America, and managed to preserve at least some of the language through song. It is only by the grace of God that this song survives along with its origin story.

Hebrews Passed Messages and History Through Song

In the Bible we often see Hebrews singing songs after miracles, battles, and for various other reasons. This has been a way for our people to pass on messages for generations. Just consider how many songs you know and understand. What we take for granted is that people outside of black culture will often know the lyrics to our music, but not the history and cultural significance of some of our music. We tend to make our music for us. Here are a few examples from scripture:

1. Moses sang after Pharaoh was drowned (Exodus 15:1).
2. Israel sang after hearing they'd receive water (Numbers 21:17).

3. God told Moses to write a song as a witness against Israel (Deuteronomy 31:19).
4. David sang when he was delivered from his enemies (2 Samuel 22:1).
5. A song of dedication at the house of David (Psalms 30:1)

Our people have always been a musical people. The more we learn about our history, the more we see that there is a very real effort to hide the truth. We are Hebrews and we were brought here on purpose.

What Did "Massa" Really Mean?

Anyone that has ever seen a movie on slavery has heard the term "massa" from a slave towards the slave owner. Many of us, including myself assumed it was because the slaves spoke broken English, which we were taught was their way of saying "master". However, when we dig into what the word means in Hebrew, there is no mistaking why they were saying "massa".

- **Massa:** Strong's # 4853 - a load, burden, lifting, bearing, tribute

If we look at the context of the situation of slavery, it would make sense that the slave owner would be referred to as a "burden". They were most certainly not paying tribute to their oppressors. While this alone isn't extremely strong evidence, in the context of the other evidence, it makes an even stronger case that enslaved black people are the Israelites of the Bible.

King Solomon's Black Lover

In the book, Song of Solomon, we are introduced to Solomon's unnamed black lover. While we don't know much about her, other than her love for the king, there are a couple of verses that stand out:

> "I am black, but comely, O ye daughters of Jerusalem, as the tents of Kedar, as the curtains of Solomon. Look not upon me, because I am black, because the sun hath looked upon me: my mother's children were angry with me; they made me the keeper of the vineyards; but mine own vineyard have I not kept." – Song of Solomon 1:5-6

Twice, Solomon's lover tells us that she is black, and she does so while making sure that we understand that's it not a metaphor or a feeling. She uses similes to describe herself:

- Black as the tents of Kedar
- Black as the tents of Solomon
- Black because of the sun

Some Eurocentric Christian doctrine attempts to explain this away as a metaphor for despair or sadness, but context proves that to be false. While we are not told her lineage, we do know that she was either a Hebrew descendant of Shem or an African descendant of Ham. This is based on the location of Israel (in Canaan), and the fact that they lived side by side with several Canaanite tribes. In addition to the unnamed black woman, Solomon also had a Hamite wife.

Pharaoh's Daughter

In ancient times, two kingdoms would often intermarry the royal sons and daughters in order to form an alliance and avoid war with each other. This was likely the case with Solomon since Israel and Egypt are next door neighbors. In addition to Pharaoh's daughter, Solomon had a list of Hamite and Hebrew women that he loved:

> "But king Solomon loved many strange women, together with the daughter of Pharaoh, women of the Moabites, Ammonites, Edomites, Zidonians, and Hittites; Of the nations concerning which the LORD said

unto the children of Israel, Ye shall not go in to them, neither shall they come in unto you: for surely they will turn away your heart after their gods: Solomon clave unto these in love." – 1 Kings 11:1-2

- Daughter of Pharaoh (descendants of Ham's son Canaan)
- Zidonians (descendants of Ham's son Canaan)
- Hittites (descendants of Ham's son Canaan)
- Moabites (Hebrew descendants of Lot)
- Ammonites (Hebrew descendants of Lot)
- Edomites (Hebrew descendants of Esau)

The women from these tribes made up Solomon's 700 wives and 300 concubines. Solomon loved many Hamite and Hebrew women, but there are no descendants of Japheth listed among the wives or concubines. Out of all of the strange women that Solomon loved, none of them stand out like his visit from the Queen of Sheba.

The Queen of Sheba

According to the Bible, The Queen of Sheba made a special trip from Ethiopia to Israel to meet Solomon, based only on hearing rumors of his wisdom. Let's look at the Queen's Hamite connection:

"And the sons of Cush; Seba, and Havilah, and Sabtah, and Raamah, and Sabtecha: and the sons of Raamah; Sheba, and Dedan." - Genesis 10:7

Sheba was the grandson of Cush and the great grandson of Ham. When the descendants of Ham began to settle Africa, Seba (son of Cush) settled the portion of Africa now known as Ethiopia. When Sheba settled, he settled in what is currently Yemen, but at the time was part of the Eastern territory controlled by Ethiopia. Sheba was essentially a city within the Ethiopian state.

The queen's name is not given in scripture, but to the Ethiopians she was known as Queen Makeda. What we do know from scripture is that she had heard the fame of Solomon and wanted to test his wisdom with "hard questions" to see if the stories were true.

"And when the queen of Sheba heard of the fame of Solomon concerning the name of the LORD, she came to prove him with hard questions." - 1 Kings 10:1

This is also reflected in the New Testament, where she is referred to as "The Queen of The South" (Luke 11:31). If we look at the map, we see that both Yemen and Ethiopia are to the south of Israel.

"The queen of the south shall rise up in the judgment with this generation, and shall condemn it: for she came from the uttermost parts of the earth to hear the wisdom of Solomon; and, behold, a greater than Solomon is here." - Matthew 12:42

Queen Makeda arrived with a massive caravan full of gifts for Solomon, even though he was already rich beyond anything mentioned in the stories she'd heard of him. After she is satisfied with his answers, The Queen of Sheba gave Solomon unmatched riches from her kingdom.

"And she gave the king an hundred and twenty talents of gold, and of spices very great store, and precious stones: there came no more such abundance of spices as these which the queen of Sheba gave to king Solomon." - 1 King 10:10

The List of Gifts

- 120 Talents of Gold
- Almug Trees
- Precious Stones
- Spices

Solomon's Gift To The Queen of Sheba

This is where the story in the Bible suddenly drops the details. After the Queen of Sheba gave Solomon his gifts, we're told the Solomon gave her all of her heart's desire, in addition to what he gave her from his royal bounty.

"And king Solomon gave unto the queen of Sheba all her desire, whatsoever she asked, beside that which Solomon gave her of his royal bounty. So she turned and went to her own country, she and her servants." - 1 Kings 10:13

Many speculate that there is a lot more to the story, and that one of her requests was a son. Let's take the following facts into consideration:

- Solomon was rich.
- Solomon was powerful.
- Solomon was wise.
- Solomon was impressive.

To think that a queen would not ask for a son with that man to secure future peace, an alliance, and a powerful son to assume the throne, would be naïve. Also, based on the fact that Solomon had 700 wives and 300 concubines, he probably wouldn't look at having a son with one more woman as a big deal. Thankfully for us, Ethiopia's well kept history picks up where the Bible leaves off.

Solomon's Secret Son

According to the *Kebra Negast* (Glory of the Kings), Queen Makeda (the Queen of Sheba) and King Solomon had a son together and his name was Menelik I (originally named Ebna la-Hakim, "Son of the Wise"). Even his name seems to suggest that there may be truth to the story. He was considered the first Solomonic emperor of Ethiopia. If the story is true, it would mean that Menelik I and his lineage were from the tribe of Judah. The Bible also makes a strange reference, but contains no explanation as to why it was made:

"Are ye not as children of the Ethiopians unto me, O children of Israel? saith the LORD. Have not I brought up Israel out of the land of Egypt? and the Philistines from Caphtor, and the Syrians from Kir?" - Amos 9:7

According to Ethiopian history, when Menelik grew up, he went to meet Solomon, was sent home with 1,000 people from each tribe (12,000 Israelites), and The Ark of The Covenant. This part of the story is why many people believe that Ethiopia is currently in possession of The Ark of The Covenant.

After returning home, Menelik I became the first leader of the Solomonic Dynasty to sit on the throne in Ethiopia. The story of the origins of Menelik I explains why Judaism and Christianity are deeply rooted in Ethiopian culture. In fact, they are so rooted in Ethiopian culture that they converted from Judaism and made Christianity their official religion 59 years before Rome. This is a fact that Eurocentric Christianity does not address in any of their teachings.

- Ethiopia converting to Christianity almost six decades before Rome is problematic for those that teach that Christianity is "the white man's religion".
- Ethiopia converting to Christianity before Rome disproves the theory that if it weren't for slavery black people wouldn't be Christians.
- Ethiopia converting to Christianity before Rome proves that it was present in Africa before the Transatlantic slave trade began.

Let's back track to The Queen of Sheba and look at her connection to Yemen.

Israelites In Yemen

There is some dispute as to whether the following pictures of Yemenite Jews taken in 1901 by Hermann Burchardt are Israelites. The following images were kept hidden away, but were released to the public on the Ha'Aretz website on May 4, 2017 under the publication title, "First-ever Photos of Yemen's Jews Stunned the Jewish World".

These people are referred to as "The Jewish community in Sana'a". What makes the images and the name of their community even more credible is that the Lemba tribe claims that their ancestors were from Sana'a and made a brief stop in Yemen, before continuing further into Africa. The Lemba claim is important because the Lemba were DNA tested and proven to be linked to the line of Levi.

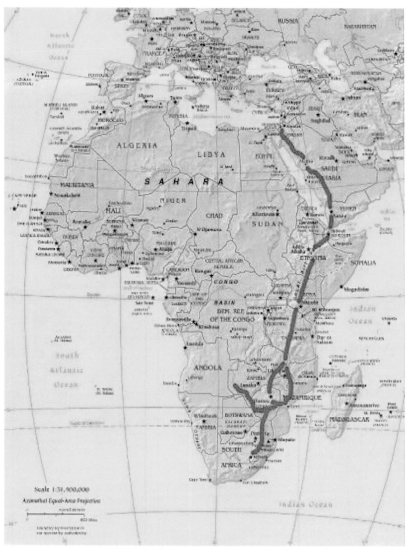

Lemba Migration Route

The connection between Israel and Ethiopia doesn't end in Africa, but extends all the way to the Caribbean, the home of Rastafarianism.

Israel Gathered From The Islands

If we look at the Transatlantic Slave Trade routes, they run through the West Indies also known as the Caribbean Islands. The Caribbean Islands are made up of Cuba, Jamaica, and Columbia to name a few.

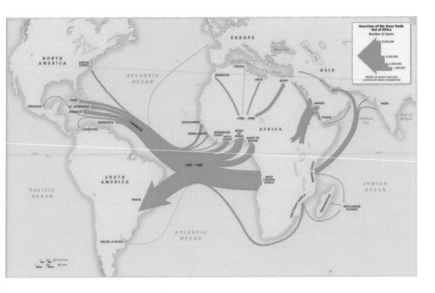

In Biblical times Ethiopia was known as "Cush" or *Kuwsh* or *Kush*, and is referenced as one of the locations from which God promised to gather Israel in the last days.

> "And it shall come to pass in that day, *that* **the Lord shall set his hand again the second time to recover the remnant of his people**, which shall be left, from Assyria, and from Egypt, and from Pathros, and **from Cush**, and from Elam, and from Shinar, and from Hamath, **and from the islands of the sea.**" - Isaiah 11:11

In addition to Ethiopia, Israel will also be gathered from "the islands of the sea", which also have a very strong connection to Ethiopia, the tribe of Judah, and King Solomon.

Rastafarian Flag – Lion of Judah

- **The Green Stripe (Top):** The beauty and vegetation of Ethiopia.
- **The Gold Stripe (Middle):** The wealth of Africa.
- **The Red Stripe (Bottom):** The blood of the martyrs.
- **The Lion:** The tribe of Judah.

Ethiopian Statue – The Lion of Judah

Emperor Haile Selassie

The reason that Rastafarians in Jamaica reference Ethiopia on their flag is directly related to the reign of Haile Selassie, the last Solomonic Emperor of Ethiopia. If there is any truth to the story that Menlik I was the son of king Solomon and Queen Makeda, it would also serve as evidence not only of a black Israel, but a strong presence of the tribe of Judah in Africa in general, and Ethiopia specifically. Because Ethiopia kept records of the Solomonic dynasty, it means we can track at least one branch of Solomon's lineage all the way to the death of Haile Selassie I in 1975.

The Ark of The Covenant

It is no secret that Ethiopia claims to be in possession of the Ark of The Covenant, and even hold a yearly procession in which they celebrate its presence. How Ethiopia came to possess the Ark of The Covenant is also directly connected to Menelik I. According to the story, Menelik I returned to Solomon as an adult, and it was he that Solomon chose to give him the Ark of The Covenant to for safe keeping.

"But through the centuries, Ethiopian Christians have claimed that the ark rests in a chapel in the small town of Aksum, in their country's northern highlands. It arrived nearly 3,000 years ago, they say, and has been guarded by a succession of virgin monks who, once anointed, are forbidden to set foot outside the chapel grounds until they die." - Smithsonian.com

If Menelik I did take the Ark of The Covenant with him for safe keeping, then it may explain why Ethiopia was never colonized like other parts of Africa.

The House of Solomon

Upon the death of Queen Makeda, Menelik I assumed the throne and began his reign around 950 BC. Ethiopia's Solomonic Dynasty continued until Emperor Haile Selassie's reign came to an end in 1974. There's no reason to believe that Ethiopia would completely fabricate their entire history, especially if everyone else in the world could visually see that they weren't Israelites. There are only two ways that this ancient claim would work:

- They were telling the truth.
- They were lying, but could pass for Israelites.

Either way, the evidence points to the Israelites being similar in skin color as Hamites. The fact that Ethiopia maintained records of the Solomonic Dynasty also adds tons of credibility to the claim. Furthermore, it gives us a glimpse into what the Hebrews actually looked like, since lineage is traced through father, and not the mother. The following lists are the Ethiopian kings lists.

The Solomonic Dynasty List

1. Emperor YəkunoAmlak (1285 – 1270)

2. Emperor YəgbaSyon (1285 -1294)
3. Emperor SeifaArəd IV (1294 -1295)
4. Emperor HəzbAsged (1295 – 1296)
5. Emperor QədmeAsged (1296 – 1297)
6. Emperor JinnAseged (1297 – 1298)
7. Emperor SabaAseged (1298 – 1299)
8. Emperor WedemArad (1299 – 1314)
9. Emperor AmdaSyon I (1314 – 1344)
10. Emperor NewayeKrəstos (1344 – 1372)
11. Emperor NewayeMaryam (1372 – 1382)
12. Emperor Dawit I (1382 – 1413)
13. Emperor Tewodros I (1413 – 1414)
14. Emperor Yəshaaq I (1414 – 1429)
15. Emperor Endryas (1429 – 1430)
16. Emperor TekleMaryam (1430 – 1433)
17. Emperor Sarwelyesus (1433)
18. Emperor AmdaIyesus (1433 – 1434)
19. Emperor ZeraaYa'əqob (1434 – 1468)
20. Emperor BeadaMaryam I (1468 – 1478)
21. Emperor Eskender (1478 – 1494)
22. Emperor AmdaSyon II (1494)
23. Emperor Na'od (1494 – 1508)
24. Emperor Dawit II (1508 – 1540)
25. Emperor Gelawdewos (1540 – 1559)
26. Emperor Menas (1559 – 1563)
27. Emperor SertseDəngəl (1563 – 1597)
28. Emperor Ya'qob (1597 – 1603)
29. Emperor ZeDəngəl (1603 – 1604)

Gonder Imperial Lineage

1. Emperor Susoneyos I (1606 – 1632)
2. Emperor Fasiledes 1632 – 1667)
3. Emperor Yohannes I (1667 – 1682)

4. Emperor Iyasu I (1682 – 1706)
5. Emperor Yshaaq Iyasu (1685)
6. Emperor TekleHaymanot I (1706 – 1708)
7. Emperor AmdaSyon (1707)
8. Emperor Tewoflos (1708 – 1711)
9. Emperor NebahneYohanns (1709 – 1710)
10. Emperor Yostos (1711 – 1716)
11. Emperor Dawit III (1716 – 1721)
12. Emperor Bakafa (1721 – 1730)
13. Emperor Iyasu II (1730 – 1755)
14. Emperor Hezqyas (1736 – 1737)
15. Emperor Iyoas I (1755 – 1769)

For those that are resistant to information from outside of the Bible, it is reasonable to believe that the Bible kept the history of the Israelites, while Ethiopians would've kept their own history. When it comes to history, the Bible is not the only source of information.

Unbelievable

In addition to all of the evidence of black Israelites in the Bible, there is even more evidence that many of the people and cultures depicted in scripture were black as well. Unfortunately, due to the white washing of history and culture by Europeans, the depiction of mostly Europeans playing historical characters, and the unwillingness of black people to openly speak out against the deception, many people find these claims unbelievable. However, the hard evidence is impossible to deny.

The following images show various cultures and individuals who have historically been depicted as white, but the evidence shows that they were indeed black. Many of these images are currently held in various museums all over the world.

From the Bristol Psalter, believed to be a Byzantine Psalter written in the 11th century in ancient Greek. The Psalter has 14 odes and the apocryphal Psalm 151. The exact provenance is unknown. Described as an Unnoticed Byzantine Psalter in a 1921 magazine article. Image f. 223r: Three Chaldean's with Israelite captives.

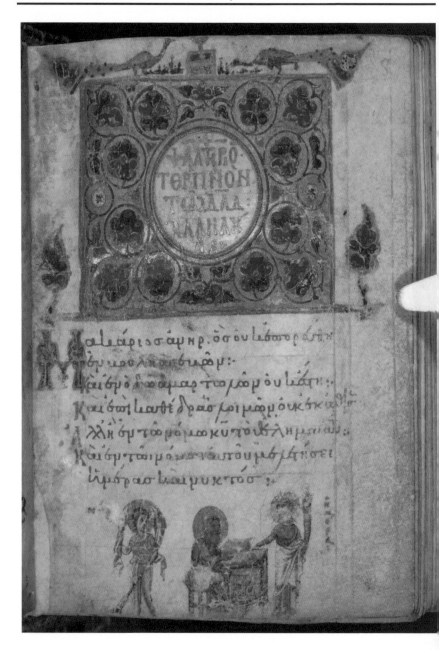

South-West palace at Nineveh, room XXXVI, panels 11-13. Mesopotamia, Neo-Assyrian era, 700-692 BC. (The British Museum, London)

Bani Rasheed (Rashaida/Rashaayda) men, Hejaz region.
From Arabia Felix: Across the Empty Quarter of Arabia by Bertram Thomas (1932)

Claim to be descendants of Abraham's grandson Kedar.

Winged sphinx from the palace of Darius the Great at Susa

"And Darius the Median took the kingdom, *being* about threescore and two years old." – Daniel 5:31

The Conception by Righteous Anna of the Most Holy Mother of God.
St. Anna, the mother of the Virgin Mary, was the youngest daughter
of the priest Nathan from Bethlehem, descended from the tribe of Levi.
She married St. Joachim, who was a native of Galilee.

Vision of John the Divine concerning Rev 1:9-20
16th c. Located at Patmos, Monastery of St. John

Christ in Majesty with symbols of the Evangelists. Illumination from a Castilian Moralia in Job, fol. 2: Spain (c. 945) Biblioteca Nacional, Madrid.

Moralia, sive Expositio in Job is the title of the commentary of Saint Gregory in the book of Job. It is also called Magna Moralia, but not to be confused with the Great Ethics of Aristotle, known by the same title.

It was written between the years 578 and 595 , when Gregory went to the court of Tiberius II in Constantinople , but was completed in Rome, after several years. This is a major work of Gregory and covers about 35 volumes, providing a comprehensive review of moral issues as the theology patristics.

Virgin Mary housed at the Jasna Góra Monastery in
Częstochowa, Poland.

Notre Dame du Puy, Cathedrale Notre Dame du Puy, Le Puy-en-Velay (Haute-Loire)
James I of Aragon in 1254 passing through Le Puy on his return from the
Holy Land, gave to the cathedral an ebony image of the Blessed Virgin clothed in
gold brocade, one of the many dozens of venerable "Black Virgins" of France:
It was destroyed in the Revolution, but replaced at the Restoration with a copy
that continues to be venerated.

Black Madonna of Czestochowa, Poland.
(Not original - Completely repainted in 1430

The Black Virgin of Montserrat: a copy at Barcelona Cathedral
The original is said to have been make by St. Luke in 54 A.D.

Our Lady of Anjony - In the chapel of the 15th century fort Château d'Anjony, France.

The Black Madonna of Einsiedeln Switzerland - 1400s

The Resurrection. Third quarter of the 16th century. The Holy Monastery of Pantokrator, Mount Athos, Greece

Pope Francis at Saint Peter's Basilica at the Vatican

The Ladder of Divine Ascent of St. John Climacus, Museum of Russian Icons, ca. 1650

Detail of Abraham and his sons including The Penitent thief (c.1600)

Moscow Temple of the Bolshoi Ordynke, celebrated in 1688.

16th century King Solomon from Vologda, Russia

Christ Pantocrator - 18th Century

Transfiguration icon by Theophanes the Greek, 15th century

inhabited by the independent tribe of the Mokteree, who have no towns, but good large villages and several strong castles. The tropical rains fall here, and consequently the country is fertile. It produces coffee, cotton, tobacco, indigo, and sesam-oil in great quantity. The Mokteree state touches the vast mountainous region of the Hojree, once a strong tribe, but now in great part subjected to the Doo Mohammed. Only a few tribes, such as the Benee Hamad, have kept their independence. This country is rich and fertile, produces coffee and cotton; the highlands may be called the home of the Kaat-tree, this precious plant growing here in greater abundance than anywhere. Here there are also mineral baths, of whose power the Arabs tell fabulous things.

The Hojree territory touches the more or less known regions of Taur, Yereem, and Ibb, and my task comes to an end here as far as regards the description of the country. I shall only add a few notes on the inhabitants, as to their mode of life, religion, and manners.

The inhabitants of this part of Arabia nearly all belong to the race of Himyar. Their complexion is almost as black as that of the Abyssinians; their bodies are very finely formed, with slender, yet strong limbs; their faces are Semitic, noses generally aquiline, eyes full of fire, lips small, and mouths of very diminutive proportions. They are generally thin, and never fat; they have little or no beard, their hair is long, but curly, not woolly.

They hardly wear any garments, nothing except a large loose cloth reaching from the waist down to the knees, and a small turban. The women have a skirt and sort of shawl. In the western district they also wear black trowsers, and in the towns a bit of cotton all over the face, without holes for the eyes.

Their only luxuries are their weapons, the long musket with the two powder-horns, and the Janbiyyah, a sort of dagger richly-ornamented with silver. Some also wear the straight sword called Nemusha.

They live in large castellated and fortified houses, three or four stories high, with towers, fortified terraces, and loopholes. The common people, however, inhabit huts of straw or palm-branches.

As to religion, the inhabitants of this part of Arabia all belong to the orthodox sect of Shafaiy. They detest the heterodox Zidiyyah of Yemen, who so long oppressed them, and the Doo Mohammed belonging to this sect. The hatred against them is general, and it is looked upon as the greatest calamity when a country is conquered by them. I cannot understand how Wellsted could believe that the inhabitants of Lahej were Zaidiyyah. They are just the

Meeting of Our Lord In The Temple

A kneeling nobleman before the Black Madonna of Einsiedeln Switzerland -1781

The Prophet Elijah's Ascent Into Heaven In The Fiery Chariot

The Holy Prophet Nahum

The Black Nazarene in the Quiapo district of the
City of Manila, Philippines.

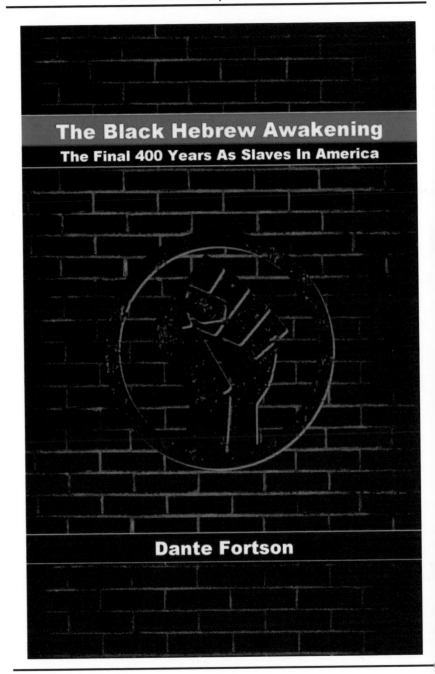

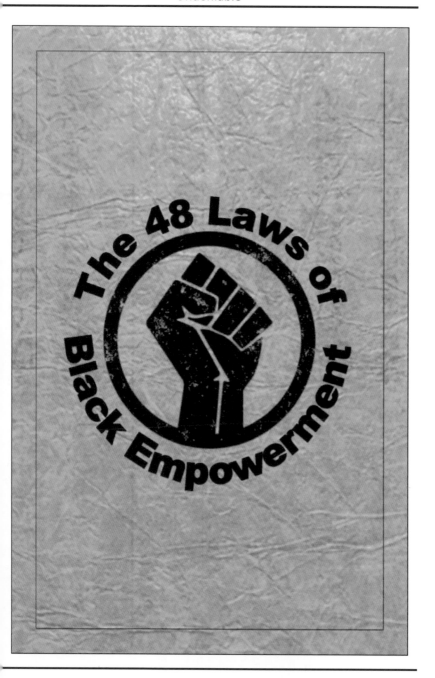

Printed in Great Britain
by Amazon

41802771R00053